LANDSCAPE
with RUINS

Margherita Guidacci. (Photo courtesy of of A. Carta.)

LANDSCAPE
with RUINS

S E L E C T E D
P O E T R Y

O F

M A R G H E R I T A
G U I D A C C I

Translated by Ruth Feldman

Introduction by Gian-Paolo Biasin

 WAYNE STATE UNIVERSITY PRESS DETROIT

Library of Congress Cataloging-in-Publication Data

Guidacci, Margherita.
Landscape with ruins : selected poetry of Margherita Guidacci/
translated by Ruth Feldman : introduction by Gian-Paolo Biasin.
p. cm.
Translated from Italian with parallel English and Italian texts
of some poems.
Includes bibliographical references.
ISBN 0-8143-2352-9 (alk. paper)
1. Guidacci, Margherita--Translations into
English. I. Feldman, Ruth. II. Title. PQ4867.U475A244 1992
851'.914--dc20   91-30227

Designer: Mary Krzewinski

Grateful acknowledgment is made to the following publications
in which some of the poems have appeared, or will be appearing:

Anthology of Magazine Verse
Ground Water Review
International Poetry Review
International Portland Review
Mundus Artium
Ploughshares
Poetry Now
Practices of the Wind
The Blue Guitar (Italy)
Webster Review

In memory of my mother
whose verses I found in a drawer after her death

Chi scrive un verso
  sa che un poeta morto
    prega per lui.

Anche sul fango
  il sole resta sole
    e non s'infanga.

Un desiderio
  e una stella cadente
    presto si spengono.

La lieve foglia
  ora forse ama il vento
    come amò l'albero.

—from *Una Breve Misura*

You who write poems
　　know somewhere a dead poet
　　　　is praying for you.

Even on the mud
　　the sun always remains sun,
　　　　never gets muddy.

A burning desire
　　and stars falling through the sky
　　　　are soon extinguished.

The inconstant leaf
　　may love the wind now as once
　　　　it adored the tree.

　　　　　　　　—from *A Brief Measure*

Contents

Contents

IV The Imminence of the Sea

CONTENTS

Translator's Note

The reader may well want to know the criteria for my selections of poems from Margherita Guidacci's many books. The factors governing my choices were twofold. First, the poet wanted examples from all of her major publications, and I was happy to concur with her wishes. Second, I chose what I considered to be the most interesting and most representative poems from each book. I am happy to say that Margherita Guidacci approved of my decisions in every case.

Incidentally, it is common practice in Italy to publish some very small volumes of a poet's work, usually, but not always, with a single theme, and to combine them later into a larger collection.

For reasons of space, it was not possible to include all of the Italian texts. I have preferred to present the reader with the widest possible sampling of Margherita Guidacci's themes and styles. I have, however, included a number of the Italian texts alongside the translations in order to give the reader a sense of the original language, its rhythms, and its particular music and timbre.

—Ruth Feldman

▼

Introduction:
A Sibyl's Voice

Biographical Notes

Born in Florence in 1921, Margherita Guidacci spent her childhood and youth in her native city, with extended summer stays in the Mugello region not far away. Both the Mugello and Florence are imbued with Renaissance and particularly Medicean memories, imprinted on the landscape as well as on many monuments, and characterized by a clarity and a serenity of contours that even today are typical of Tuscany—and that are to be found at the core of Guidacci's poetical language and choices.

Soon after graduating from the University of Florence with a thesis on the early poetry of Giuseppe Ungaretti, Guidacci started a prolific career as translator, essayist, and poet. Her first translations into Italian of John Donne and Max Beerbohm date back to 1946, the same year as her first collection of poems, *La sabbia e l'angelo*, and were followed by translations of the work of T. S. Eliot (1947), Emily Dickinson (1947, 1961, and 1979), Ezra Pound (1958), Archibald MacLeish (1958), Henry James (1960), Joseph Conrad (1962 and 1963), Mark Twain (1962), Edith Louise Sitwell (1968 and 1989), Christopher Smart (1975), Jessica Powers (1982), Sarah Orne Jewett (1983), and Ruth Feldman (1989). She also translated British religious plays (1950) and Irish popular tales (1961) and, from other languages, Sophocles (1958), ancient Chinese tales (1959), Jorge Guillén (1960), Tao Huang Ming (1965 and 1970), Mao Tse-tung (1973), an anthology of Estonian poets (1973), and the writings of

15

Pope John Paul II (1979 and 1981). This list is impressive because it shows the range of Guidacci's knowledge and interests: not only poetry but also fiction, not only personal lyricism but also epic narration—and, in particular, a religiosity that is open to both classic British plays and the strict Catholicism of the pope. These interests nourish her poetry as well.

As a critic, Guidacci wrote remarkable studies on T. S. Eliot (1947–75) and American poets and narrators (1978), and she has contributed to numerous Italian journals and papers, including the authoritative Vatican daily *L'Osservatore Romano*. She lives in Rome, where she teaches English literature in a private college.

Tradition and Modernity

Margherita Guidacci's formation is distinguished by her independence and uniqueness from a very early age; she herself has said that she owed something to Nicola Lisi, an elegant but simple and intensely religious Tuscan narrator, who was her mother's cousin; Giuseppe Ungaretti, one of the great poets of the Italian twentieth century, who was called "hermetic" for the difficulty many critics encountered in deciphering his poems, which were constructed on a few, essential words; and Giuseppe De Robertis, the Florentine literary critic who taught a rigorous attention to stylistic features and values to generations of Italians. Yet it is appropriate to say that though she was nourished by them, she was not really influenced by Lisi, Ungaretti, and De Robertis—nor, for that matter, by the other Tuscan and religious poet, Mario Luzi, sometimes mentioned in connection with her work.

Guidacci has undoubtedly learned from the religiosity of Lisi and Clemente Rebora, the essentiality of Ungaretti and Eugenio Montale, and the rigor of De Robertis and Eliot, but what she has learned has become unequivocally hers, and from the very beginning her poetry could not be said to be hermetic or any other adjective used to label one or another poetical school. There are, for example, many

"Montalean" words in Guidacci's poems, such as *sunflower*, *weathervane*, or *agave*, but, as soon as the reader recognizes them, she or he also notices how different they are; they have lost all the qualities and connotations and meanings that were Montale's and have acquired entirely original meanings, connotations, and qualities that are Guidacci's own, solely and distinctly.

In any case, Guidacci refused to write in ways that would smack of "sophistication," wanted to keep her words as simple and plain as possible, and wanted her poetry to be as natural as it could be—that is, she wanted to write a "poetry of experience" based on signifieds and not on the play of signifiers and always sought to find and render in her poetic language the adherence of words to things, the *adequatio rei et intellectus*. Two general corollaries derive from these premises. First, her poems seem to be (and to a certain extent are) easier to read and understand than many avant-garde texts played almost entirely on formal qualities. Second, her poems are mostly based on a free or blank verse that is close to narration (with the notable exception of her Italian haiku texts, modeled after the Japanese genre and published under the title *Una breve misura, A Brief Measure*).

But the seeming naturalness and simplicity of Guidacci's poetry should not be taken lightly; it should not be oversimplified or overnaturalized. Her poetry is imbued with a religiosity and compassion that transcend her personal self (even when she talks about herself and the terrifying experience of a psychic sickness, as in her collection *Neurosuite*, for example, or of the loss of a beloved person as in *A Farewell*) and point to a very high conception of poetry and its function.

For Guidacci, poetry is the human voice that witnesses human destiny in its broadest manifestations (history and nature) as well as in its innermost nuances (love or fear, beauty or disgust). In its witnessing, poetry discovers the traces of the divine in all the cracks and voids of the world, and it relies on the maternal, earthy solidity of its origin, shrouded in darkness, to achieve light. The light, indeed the splendor, of Guidacci's poetry is the revelation at the

17

same time of infinity—a religious feeling—and the limitation of language to express such an infinity—pathos, a poetical feeling.

In the background of Guidacci's poetics there are, of course, general traces of the great Italian tradition dating back to the Middle Ages of Dante, Saint Francis of Assisi, and Jacopone. But, more particularly, Guidacci is imbued with another Italian tradition—from Ugo Foscolo's *Dei sepolcri* to Giacomo Leopardi's *La ginestra*, to cite the two great Romantic poets whose themes, more directly than the Catholic Alessandro Manzoni's, might be traced in her work. And she is also linked to an extra-Italian tradition, from the ancient Greek Sophocles to the American Emily Dickinson, representing the appeal of the epic and of the personal, respectively, and the great British metaphysical poetry of the seventeenth century should not be forgotten, nor the influence of Eliot and Gerard Manley Hopkins.

But Guidacci is also profoundly modern, especially in her insisted-on consciousness of the contrast between the infinity perceived and the limitation of language to express it. This contrast is particularly evident and touching in those poems (such as in *Book of Stars*) in which she speaks with a voice that is close to nature—the universe, the starred sky, and the earth—as the impassive companion of humans, with their deeds and their destinies, and even more so in those poems, such as in *A Book of Sibyls*, in which she speaks with the voice of the Sibyls, those prophetesses of the ancient world, and transforms centuries of sorrows, defeats, and deaths into the incredible serenity and luminosity of a comprehensive and almost totalizing vision.

To Guidacci the Sibyls "represent a very ancient and primitive form of cult, bound to the earth and to the vital forces that issue from it"; "similar to the Goethian [and, we should add, Jungian] 'mothers' . . . they guard an enigma that is close, however, to the heart of life, to which the woman is perhaps more intimately connected than the man, and succeeds better, therefore, in plumbing it" *A Book of Sibyls*, 57). This is a very important explanation because it takes us to the very core of her poetry (and of feminine poetry in general?). Unlike the poetry of poet-bards like Giosuè Carducci or Gabriele D'Annunzio, based on historical certitudes and national, even nationalistic, values (with the inevitable, masculine tinge associated with such certitudes and values), Guidacci's poetry is the epic voice not of a single bard but of many Sibyls, who express the values of human destiny, not those of human history, and are unified in their recognizable plurality—another modern trait—by their common compassion and far-reaching vision. Or perhaps no: Guidacci simply rescues the lost voices of the Sibyls and restores their fragments to the great level of the bards—Homer, Foscolo, Walt Whitman.

An Anthology: Themes and Images

An anthology is always a matter of choosing what an interpreter considers essential in the oeuvre to be presented, an operation whose risks are at least as high as the merits to be reaped. A certain amount of subjectivity is in fact inevitable even in the most detached and objective approach, and the regret for what is left out may undermine the very persuasiveness of the presentation. In the case of this anthology I believe that the risks have been minimized by two factors: the uniformly high tone of Guidacci's poetry and Ruth Feldman's inner consonance with the Italian poet, so that each fragment, each selected poem, represents the whole work in both an objective and subjective way—or may be said to be a microcosm that reveals and conveys the sense of the entire oeuvre.

Let me give a very persuasive example. The first poem selected for this anthology sets the tone of the entire book and expresses the essential characteristic of Guidacci's poetry:

Chi grida sull'alto spartiacque è udito da entrambe le valli.
Perciò la voce dei poeti intendono i viventi ed i morti.

The one who calls out on the high divide is heard from
   both valleys.
Thus the voice of the poets is heard by the living and the
   dead.

It is a beautiful poem, a programmatic statement that truly defines Guidacci's conception of poetry in a way that is reminiscent of Ugo Foscolo's meditation on the tombs and, more recently, Walter Benjamin's idea that the authority of a narrator derives from speaking from the point of view of death. This authority makes possible the dialogue of the poet with both the living and the dead. The great divide between life and death is indeed the privileged viewpoint from which Guidacci is able to look at human destiny with the intensity, the immediacy, and the metaphysical awe that are so characteristic of her poetry. Sorrow, joy, solitude, love, the passing of time, the violence of history, all can be witnessed by the far-reaching vision of the poet, which ultimately corresponds perfectly and almost naturally with that of the Sibyls.

If the theme of death, then, should be considered fundamental in the very organization of Guidacci's poetry, the theme of life is equally basic, and a third concern becomes immediately thematized as well: "the voice of the poets," the nature of poetry. Guidacci is quite conscious of her poetic voice and never tires of highlighting it with a self-referential attitude, which is, however, unfettered by intellectualistic preoccupations and is developed in beautiful images. Finally, the "high divide" and the "valleys" of the initial line of the poem point out another fundamental aspect of Guidacci's poetry: her interest in the landscape— a landscape that is both physical and metaphysical, as it is here, or one that is both natural and historical, inhabited by generations of men and women who have left their traces on it before disappearing: precisely a "landscape with ruins," as stated in the beautiful title Feldman has chosen for this volume.

I have no intention of anthologizing this anthology by selecting passages, lines, or poems that seem particularly beautiful or meaningful to me. Rather, I wish to point out some itineraries that may be followed in reading these poems—itineraries that are already imbedded in the text and need only to be opened up. The notion of an itinerary is mainly spatial, taking a person from one place to another, and only secondarily temporal, indicating the time necessary to travel between the two points. And this is exactly what I have in mind as a possible critical description of Guidacci's poetry, which is structured according not to successive phases in time but to variations and probes into different directions within its space. Hence it would be useless to look for developments and changes from one collection of verse to the next.

These reading itineraries essentially correspond to three major themes. The first and most evident is the theme of death, stated as early as 1946 in a poem from *The Sand and the Angel,* in which the "little" death of the single individual is projected against the "great" death of an entire civilization and universalized by the pronoun "we":

Non occorrevano i templi in rovina sul limitare di
   deserti. . . .
Bastava che l'ombra sorgesse dall'angolo più quieto della
   stanza . . .
La fine pioggia ai vetri, un pezzo di latta che gemesse nel
   vento:
Noi sapevamo già di appartenere alla morte.

We didn't need the crumbling temples on the deserts'
   edge. . . .
It was enough that the shadow rose from the quietest
   corner of the room . . .
The fine rain against the windowpanes, a piece of tin
   moaning in the wind:
We knew already we belonged to death.

Our belonging to death is explored and expressed throughout Guidacci's oeuvre, but especially in the poems of *A Farewell,* in which the private death of a beloved person is objectified in beautiful images of stars and ice, and *The Bologna Clock,* in which the public deaths of the most horrible terrorist attack in recent Italian history are lamented and sublimated through a Biblical language that places them in a superior perspective, without renouncing an iota of civic indignation. In particular the subject of death is central to *A Book of Sibyls* and *Rings of Time,* the most recent collections (the first published and the other in progress), in which the awareness of death is shared with the whole of humanity, from the high divide of poetry that joins the modern Sibyl with the ancient prehistoric inhabitants of the "Cueva de las Manos."

The second itinerary is that of life. It goes from the tormented pages of *Neurosuite*, expressing the anguish and fear of the experience of a mental sickness, with such tale-telling images as a "desert of lava," a moth "walled up in centuries of amber," or the two "silent aquariums" of the sane and the sick facing each other, to the splendid items of *Slavic Notebook*, such as the cock of the homonymous poem, which is "bigger than the village," "bigger than the entire countryside," because its voice is so all-embracing that "even the sun . . . is only the fiery eye of a cock!" This itinerary culminates in the poems of *Hymn to Joy* (the Bee-thoven-inspired title is the only one apt to describe a love experience that is capable of reclaiming the moon to the territory of feelings—and poetry) and *Book of Stars*, in which the starry sky becomes the mirror, the objective correlative of an inner sky, reflecting love and compassion, serenity and beauty.

The third itinerary is particularly clear in *Emptiness and Forms*, in which poetry is indeed the force bridging the existential void and capable of rising from its ashes like a phoenix, and *The Isenheim Altar*, a description of Mathias Grünewald's altarpiece, which is a metonymic description of poetry's own procedures, themes, and forms. But the self-awareness necessary to talk about art is in fact present throughout the volume (the itineraries I propose do inter-sect and overlap), and I would choose the poem "Winter" from *Slavic Notebook* as a case in point:

Soltanto se intervenga l'occhio
e l'anima e la mano del pittore,
questo stesso paesaggio sarà la nostra orma,
diverrà il nostro volo incancellabile.

Only if the painter's eye,
heart and hand intervene,

22

will this same landscape be our track,
become our ineffaceable flight.

Indeed, the book of nature must be deciphered by human
readers who know its alphabet, otherwise the landscape
remains a blank page. But deciphering is not enough; there
must be total intervention involving the eye, heart and
mind of the artist in order to transform the natural land-
scape into a human art-ifact: a painting or a poem. And it is
the flight of art that is ineffaceable, while the great monu-
ments of human power—walls or palaces or temples—may
crumble, and there will be left only a landscape with ruins.

The Translation

Undoubtedly Ruth Feldman is the most perfectly suited
translator for the poems of Margherita Guidacci, with
whom she has a consonance that is much deeper than I
implied earlier on. In her own right Feldman is a poet and
a painter as well (this biographical datum, incidentally, may
help to account for some of the choices of poems for this
anthology, such as the ten dedicated to Grünewald's altar-
piece). Her poems, which Guidacci herself translated into
Italian with the title *Perdere la strada nel tempo* (*Losing Your
Way in Time*), show many of the themes we have seen in
Guidacci's poetry: a sense of death and the inexorable
passing of time, the joys and sorrows of life, a painter's eye
for the landscape and a self-conscious appreciation of art,
and the detachment and the compassion of a Sibyl-like long
view of human destiny. Feldman regularly spends part of
her life in Italy, whose art, history, and people she knows
and loves as few others do. She has translated many italian
poets into English—Vittorio Bodini, Bartolo Cattafi, Primo
Levi, Lucio Piccolo, Rocco Scotellaro, and Andrea Zanzotto,
just as Guidacci translated many American authors into
Italian. In short, the artistic encounter between Feldman
and Guidacci could not have occurred under better auspi-
ces.

The results are evident for every reader to see and appre-
ciate. The poems selected and presented in this anthology

are beautiful English poems that have preserved not only the compassion and wisdom but also the solemn and yet soft-voiced tone of the original text, which, on occasion, Feldman has included here—its ample and flowing rhythm, its elegant syntax balanced between the classic and the discursive, and its simple yet inspired lexicon. The "mode of signification" of the original has been, as Benjamin would say, "lovingly and in detail" incorporated by and in this translation.

If to translate can mean, etymologically, to carry across, Feldman has indeed carried Guidacci's texts across the Atlantic, and across the linguistic barrier, into the landscape of contemporary American poetry. And hers, like Guidacci's, is truly a Sibyl's voice. May its echo linger long in our time.

Gian-Paolo Biasin
University of California at Berkeley

I

BETWEEN
STONE
AND
STREAM

MEDITATIONS AND MAXIMS

I

The one who calls out on the high divide is heard from both
    valleys.
Thus the voice of the poets is heard by the living and the
    dead.

IV

A few drops of dew revive the short grass
To the patience of another dry day;
The parched tree longs for rain or the axe.

V

This is the way the world's divided; in the beginning is the
    breeze;
Then there are the things responding to the breeze, in sound
    or movement.
There is also the cruel stone that breaks the breeze's flight
And on which nothing that responds to the breeze can
    germinate.

XIV

The man the breeze chose for companion
Will erect in vain a hedge or wall against it.
For him, the breeze's voice will be preserved by silence
As in a shell, and rejected, will sound more loudly in his
    heart
Until he rises up and follows it.

XIX

The mouths of rivers are sources of the sea, the sea a source
Of clouds, the clouds sources of sources. In this way
Space and time move in sure rings around us
Until changeless eternity reigns.

XXI

Every death contains all of earth's death.
Therefore, dying you will know
The fish hurled ashore in the night of hurricane,
The burnt tree, the wild beast brought low by hunger,
And the long sleep of destroyed peoples
Under the sands of forgotten kingdoms.

XXIV

Don't ask the flame to save you from the night.
In the circle of shadow and howls
Its reflection will dance in the eye of the lurking wolf;
Grim birds, disturbed
By the redness that destroys the moth
Will beat their wings more madly on your face.
The flame was placed there as a sign
For your heart only. Leap and tremble with it
Until day dawns.

La Sabbia e l'angelo

I

Non occorrevano i templi in rovina sul limitare di deserti,
Con le colonne mozze e le gradinate che in nessun luogo
conducono;
Né i relitti insabbiati, le ossa biancheggianti lungo il mare;
E nemmeno la violenza del fuoco contro i nostri campi e le
case.
Bastava che l'ombra sorgesse dall'angolo più quieto della
stanza
O vegliasse dietro la nostra porta socchiusa—
La fine pioggia ai vetri, un pezzo di latta che gemesse nel
vento:
Noi sapevamo già di appartenere alla morte.

V

Furono ultime a staccarsi le voci. Non le voci tremende
Della guerra e degli uragani,
E nemmeno voci umane ed amate,
Ma mormorii d'erbe e d'acque, risa di vento, frusciare
Di fronde tra cui scoiattoli invisibili giocavano,
Ronzìo felice d'insetti attraverso molte estati
Fino a quell'insetto che più insistente ronzava
Nella stanza dove noi non volevamo morire.
E tutto si confuse in una nota, in un fermo
E sommesso tumulto, come quello del sangue
Quando era vivo il nostro sangue. Ma sapevamo ormai
Che a tutto ciò era impossibile rispondere.
E quando l'Angelo ci chiese: «Volete ancora ricordare?»
Noi stessi l'implorammo: «Lascia che venga il silenzio!»

The Sand and the Angel

I

We didn't need the crumbling temples on the deserts' edge,
With lopped columns and stairs that lead nowhere;
Nor the sand-covered wreckage, the bleached bones along the
    sea.
Not even the violence of fire against our fields and homes.
It was enough that the shadow rose from the quietest corner
    of the room
Or kept its vigil behind our half-closed door—
The fine rain against the windowpanes, a piece of tin
    moaning in the wind:
We knew already we belonged to death.

V

The voices were the last to go. Not the terrible voices
Of war and hurricanes;
Not even human loved voices,
But murmurs of grass and water, wind's laughter, rustling
Of branches among which invisible squirrels played,
Happy buzzing of insects in the course of many summers
Until that insect buzzing more insistently
In the room where we did not want to die.
And it all merged into one note, into a steady
Subdued noise like that of blood,
When our blood was alive. But we knew by now
It was impossible for us to respond.
And when the Angel asked us: "Do you still want to
    remember?"
We ourselves implored him: "Let the silence come!"

ALL SAINTS' DAY

I

All Saints' Day; November sky
Reflected in the streets' rain-soaked
Asphalt, two parallel grays
To oppress the glance
Wherever it seeks escape. The city
Seems lead and ash, and the raw
Flash of headlights turns pedestrians'
Faces still more ghostly. The hours
Glide by slowly in this roar of water,
Between short splashes of mud
And the whirling of rotten leaves
From gardens. It's hard today
To think of Paradise; everything
Brings us back and drags us down to earth.
There's too much faith needed to leap
Sorrow's high barrier. It will, instead,
Be easy tomorrow, in the wake
Of a disintegrating season,
To remember the end of all flesh.

III

I have often thought: this is
The year's real end and Apocalypse
With its brown and gray, two empty bezels,
All the colored gems that stared at us
Before, extinguished. The world is
Dissolved in these rotten ferments
Of death. The water carries the earth
Away from the mountains, leaving
The stones naked, the wind carries the leaves away
Until the final dryness of the trees.
Nothing remains but to hope
For the time when there will no longer
Be anything to lose. Already under
The anguish of flesh the skeleton
Shows and reaffirms the harsh
And patient wait.

                                        This is
The end, not December with crystal
Skies, the Star of the East
And men kneeling to adore
The Child. In silence—though
Hidden from the world—hope will revive
With the seed under the snow.
                                        But twice
In these days when earth itself
Resembles a scene from the Last Judgment
He who will return is recalled
To us from the altar: no longer a child
To save us, but an adult to judge
The quick and the dead, to exclude
Any new redemption. Then time's hinges
Will turn, huge and bleak,
And eternity shall be. You alone, Saints,
Will dare to gaze at it.

                                        V

I have many memories of November: too many times now
The sky's cold Sagittarius has drawn his bow
Over my life. And I find again many things in the past
With an intense meaning they didn't have at the time,
Or that I didn't see. Days
Of adolescence and the short vacations
At the beginning of this month: I roamed
The countryside, among damp leaves.
It was fun to trample and kick them
Ahead of me, heedless then
As the wind. I searched for ferns
On the paths' edge, happy
With their bitter scent, their varied
Designs. I saw reddish bushes
Pale little by little to inert gray,
Hailed the first ice-star that appeared
On a mud puddle. In the stinging air,
Where every bird-cry was a blade,
I exulted—more than under a summer sun—in my
Freedom . . .

                Then came a wartime November.
Streams fell from the mountains,
Covering the streets where tanks
Of three foreign armies in pursuit
Dug deadly ruts, often debouching
Into bomb craters. In the invaded land,
Among people bent and scattered
Under the storm, impending winter
Bared the depths of every evil . . .
                        Later I found myself
One November far from my country:
I see again the deserted
Beach at Howth, a somber sky,
And the sparse and livid gleam there
Seemed to rise
From under the sea, like a malevolent
Thought that leaped suddenly
From a heart without peace . . .

II

A
WALLED-IN
BUTTERFLY

From *Neurosuite*

SALA D'ATTESA

In fondo ai loro occhi
si accendono fiammelle di terrore
o si stende una fredda
e rassegnata nebbia.

I loro pensieri si srotolano
come bende sfrangiate ed infette
(acre il sentore,
appiccicoso il tatto,
fa ribrezzo tentare
di rimetterle a posto.)

Per tenere a distanza il dolore
(come se ormai non lo portassero in sé!)
giocano con un soprammobile,
guardano i quadri alle pareti,
prendono un rotocalco e si concentrano
sforzandosi di credere che tutto il mondo si regga
su qualche nuova marca di rossetto
o sul punteggio d'una squadra di calcio.

Finché la porta che per tutto il tempo
senza parere han sorvegliato, s'apre.
Sono chiamati ed entrano e ricevono
tutto il conforto che di là era in serbo:
un nome greco per il loro male.

Waiting Room

Deep in their eyes
small flames of terror are lit
or a cold resigned mist
spreads.

Their thoughts unroll
like frayed polluted bandages
(sour-smelling,
sticky to the touch;
it's revolting to try
to put them back in place).

To keep pain at a distance
(as if by now they didn't carry it inside themselves)
they play with knickknacks,
stare at the paintings on the walls,
pick up a picture magazine and concentrate on that,
struggling to believe the whole world hangs
on some new brand of lipstick
or a soccer team's score.

Until the door they've watched the whole time,
without seeming to, opens.
They're summoned, enter, and receive
all the comfort that was in store for them:
a Greek name for what ails them.

To Doctor Z

Gazing at our far-off planet
with your crude telescope
you lavish kindly advice upon us:
"You're in the sea; save yourselves by swimming!"
Not understanding
that the sea you perceive from that distance
is a rippling desert of lava
solidified on top of us as it is
on Vesuvius's ancient dead.
And you persist: "Why aren't you moving?
A few strokes and you'll reach shore!"
Would you counsel flying
to a moth walled up
in centuries of amber?

A Clinical Case

Flattering to feel yourself a textbook case,
to be sure others will learn
from the intervals of your agony
and its rekindling.

To know that the Galaxy of your corpuscles
will fill maps of consultation
and the Nijinsky of your nerves will keep on dancing
even when the curtain falls.

Don't turn so distractedly
to dull health and to your onetime home.
Frost will cover you like a glory
when the time comes.

ORA DEL PASSO

Attesa di visitatori,
desiderio che vengano,
poi vano tentativo
di dare e di ricevere parole
oltre il muro di vetro che separa
i due mondi e li rende
l'uno per l'altro un muto acquario.

Effimero sollievo degli addii
subito rinnegato
dal pensoso affacciarsi sulla scala
seguendo con lo sguardo
chi già vorresti richiamare e non osi
(se ritorna, di nuovo ti ritrai).

La porta oscilla nei due sensi,
sempre sulla medesima tristezza
e tu non sai se la vuoi aperta o chiusa:
tu cui la solitudine
è la peggiore compagnia
come la compagnia
è la peggior solitudine.

Visiting Hour

Waiting for visitors,
wanting them to come,
then a futile attempt
to give and receive words
outside the glass wall that separates
the two worlds and makes them into
a silent aquarium for each other.

Fleeting relief of the good-byes,
immediately denied
by the wistful gazing from the landing,
following with your glance
the ones you would already like to call back
but don't dare to
(if they do return, you withdraw all over again).

The door swings two ways,
always on the same sadness,
and you don't know whether you want it
open or closed:
you, for whom solitude
is the worst company,
as company
is the worst solitude.

Psycho-Tests

They dream up crafty questions,
count the yeses and the nos,
and judge us from those
as though they were the Lord.

We judge them too;
their net is so stupid
that, even feeling we are caught in it,
we don't bother to tear loose

but leave them to the proud delusion
that they have achieved a great result
if someone who knows nothing
about himself, about existence,
distinguishes a rhomb from a square.

The Mad Mother

With the cast-off rags of the past
we build ourselves a present,
clutch it to our chests
like a doll filled with sawdust,
cradle it tenderly.
Just so, the mad mother, my neighbor,
talks to a little boy
who disappeared long ago among the flowers,
and meanwhile turns her back indignantly
on the gray man, flabby and broken,
that little boy has become,
and who begs her in vain
to recognize him.

For Us No Mirror

For us no mirror,
faithful or distorting.
No pools of tremulous water,
no shop windows for a furtive glance.

The *gnothi seautón* is defeated
by a total lack of reflections.
Grayness of walls, of asphalt,
of dense fog.

Cut off from knowledge, now we search
only for the key of ignorance.
Has the world become all that opaque
or have we no faces anymore?

FEAR

My fear is compact, a thick-furred beast
that unsheathes and retracts its claws,
stretches out against the doors I'd like to open
and squeezes under the ones
I'd like to keep closed. It walks furtively
like a great cat, leaps on my chest at night
and makes my dreams a mixture of suffocating grips
and hot damp breath, from which I wake sweat-soaked.
It walks beside me, more faithful than my shadow,
because unlike my shadow, it knows no rest,
stares at me red-eyed in the middle of the night.
We are bound to each other forever;
neither of us can break loose.
We've tamed each other; it no longer
attacks me unexpectedly,
but only follows with deadly patience.
I no longer struggle to drive it away, but take refuge
in a cramped corner of my mind
where even day is obscured by woolly clouds
that no rain dissolves, no purifying wind scatters:
dark fermenting mass before which I bend lower and lower
in my shrinking corner, until I almost merge with earth
where everything, even fear, will cease to be.

A Clockless Land

"A clockless land"—or perhaps too many of them,
all contradictory, so that we decided
to forget the foolish tangle of their hands,
to do away with their faces,
burying them under the snow,
and to regulate our lives, or what
we called our lives, by the variations
(for that matter highly improbable)
of our empty sky,
and by the footstep—very sure—
of the Stranger who continued to approach
behind us.

WALLED

Walled into words
or walled into silence
(silence a white wall,
words a multicolored one)
all we could hear
in the adjoining cell
was the other person's heart—
mournful metronome.
Often we couldn't hear
even those beats
and we were never sure
the rhythm synchronized with ours.

THE BEECHES OF KOZJAK

If these beeches knew all that we know,
a premature autumn would redden them,
fever would dart with the wind in the foliage;
they would be gnawed by our heart's wicked worm.

If we knew what the beeches know,
we would rise calm on the banks of Kozjak.
Birds with white and black wings
would fly to us without fear.
We would be reborn each dawn to innocence,
each night to lofty contemplation:
above us the stars
and the footsteps of the gods.

Proščansko Jezero

Floating on the cool waters of Prošče,
from the top of this water tower
I let my thoughts descend
through fifteen lakes.

Here, where if I died, no one would ever find me,
where I myself do not distinguish my identity
from the cry of a solitary bird,
the swaying of a lakeside reed,
here where everything is a quiet shimmer,

still I feel drawn downward
by long and steady
threads of water
through a needle-eye of rock,

and I am like the fugitive Korana,
seeking plains and cities,
with human footsteps sounding on its banks,
boys leaning on the parapets of bridges,
murmurs of love on the shingle,
laughter, sobbing and quarrels,
and all the brotherly chaos
to which I still belong.

GLI AMANTI

Gli amanti stanno distesi, uno a fianco dell'altro,
e somigliano ai morti: totale è l'abbandono
non a Eros né a Hypnos
ma a Thanatos, il genio che presiede alla Morgue,
di cui il letto ripete la fredda lastra orizzontale.
Che pietà delle giovani teste arrovesciate,
come sono esangui, indifese le membra!
Ho paura dei tuoi sogni, eppure non riesco
a mormorare una preghiera, fratello.
Perché il tuo mondo è fatto di grigie ragnatele
che coprono i fanciulli;
sui muri si rincorrono le ombre
in disperati carnevali;
di qua e di là dalle finestre il vuoto
è minaccioso come una presenza
e lampade che ardono soltanto per se stesse
fanno più fondo il buio negli occhi di chi guarda.
Tu che hai dipinto queste scene e conoscevi l'inferno
potevi trarne un canto d'amore? Solo il silenzio,
puro più d'ogni canto ti ravvolge.
Io non so la natura del sasso che cadde nell'acqua profonda,
ma con ansioso cuore lo seguo fino all'ultimo cerchio.

The Lovers

The lovers lie, one at the other's side,
resembling the dead; their yielding is total,
not to Eros or to Hypnos
but to Thanatos, the genius who presides over the Morgue,
whose bed the cold flat slab repeats.
How pitiful the young heads, thrown back,
how bloodless and defenseless the limbs!
I am afraid of your dreams, brother,
and yet I can't murmur a prayer.
Because your world is made of gray cobwebs
that envelop the children;
on the walls the shadows chase each other
in desperate carnivals;
inside and outside the windows the void
is menacing as a presence,
and lamps that burn for themselves alone
deepen the darkness in the beholders' eyes.
You, who painted these scenes and knew hell,
could you draw from it a love song? Only silence,
purer than any song, enshrouds you.
I do not know the nature of the stone
that fell into deep water, but with a troubled heart
I follow it to the very last circle.

GALLO

Il gallo è più grande del villaggio,
è più grande del bosco,
più grande della campagna,
perché la sua voce tutto riempie, tutto abbraccia.
Ogni cosa su cui cadon le sue note
deve per forza rispondere.
Il nostro sangue gira impazzito
col segnavento della torre (che ha immagine di gallo)
ogni cespuglio fiorito rivela
colori e curvatura di una coda di gallo;
perfino il sole, levandosi sul monte,
è soltanto l'occhio ardente di un gallo!

Cock

To Ivan Lacković

The cock is bigger than the village,
bigger than the woods,
bigger than the entire countryside,
because his voice fills and embraces everything.
Wherever his notes fall
an answer must spring up.
Our blood whirls in a frenzy
with the tower's weathervane (shaped like a cock);
every flowering bush reveals
colors and curves like a cock's tail;
even the sun, rising over the mountain,
is only the fiery eye of a cock!

WINTER

To Ivan Lacković

On this soft whiteness
tracks are easily imprinted,
still more easily erased.

Clearcut the black flights of birds
in the snowfilled air,
but they too are an alphabet that quickly vanishes,
the page turns white again.

Only if the painter's eye,
heart and hand intervene,
will this same landscape be our track,
become our ineffaceable flight.

Nothing else is needed, Ivan, and you know it.
Really nothing else.

EMPTINESS AND FORMS

The pursuit, the struggle
on the invisible brink,
the images seized, believed to be
already ours, and in an instant
turning again to mist,
the frustrated return—
of the hunter who reaped only
a swish of twigs and the brief gray flash
of the hare bounding to safety among the bushes;
of the fisherman whose long wait
ended in an ironical flicker of carp,
that silver mockery over the barely grazed hook . . .

How distressed we are.
How our useless weapons drop from our hands.
Stone remains stone,
canvas is only canvas, the sheet of paper
a rustling absence, the keyboard
stubborn silence.

Emptiness defends itself.
It doesn't want to be tortured into form.

IL MURO E IL GRIDO

Hanno chiuso le porte—
grevi porte ferrate—
tirato i chiavistelli,
rinforzato le spranghe.

Perché non esca il grido,
perché gli altri non sappiano,
han fatto un muro, lungo
quanto il mare e le Ande.

Ma il sangue impregna il muro,
cola sotto le porte.
Se i morti hanno la bocca sigillata
gridano dalle vene aperte,

in ogni vena grida
la libertà trucidata.
La terra insonne ode
solo il grido, il grido.

The Wall and the Cry

They have closed the doors—
heavy ironclad doors—
shot the bolts home,
reinforced the bars.

So that the cry will not escape,
so that the others will not know,
they have built a wall, long
as the sea and the Andes.

But blood soaks the wall,
trickles under the doors.
If the dead have their mouths sealed
they will scream from open veins.

In every vein
murdered liberty groans.
The sleepless earth hears
only the cry, the cry.

Your Violated House

to Pablo Neruda, after his death

Your violated house, the broken bits
of glass, of shells (cutting edges),
the torn drawings, splintered masks
that stare
with twice blind eyes . . .
Why so much abuse? A dead man
is not hated like this!

Not a dead man, but a living one. That is
the answer their instinct has supplied,
infallible, as in all wild beasts.
Dazzling, tremendous
is your life, Pablo.
And above the pyre they have readied
for your poems, shines
your unconsumed phoenix nature.

The Water Complains

The water complains:
I'm thirsty! I'm thirsty!
I'm burned
by rank slime,
by the verdigris of acids.
I'm suffocated
by bloated dead fish.
Big thorns
of rusty iron
prick my soft throat.
A dull fever
consumes me.
Give me, I beg of you,
a drop . . . of what?

Of what? This is the truly
insoluble problem!
How can we quench our thirst
if even the water is thirsty?

THE ROAD, THE RIVER

Sheltered in her house, in its most tranquil room,
with all her favorite knickknacks round her,
suddenly she feels the road open,
the river flow.

When talking with her friends,
before the answer to a simple question comes to her,
and with the teaspoon halfway to her lips,
she knows the road can open,
the river flow.

While she is reading silently at night,
the gap between line and line the eyes traverse
and the interval when the page is turned
become a road that opens,
a rushing river.

Who will save her if, seemingly, nothing has changed?
Who will catch her on the invisible brink?
She was here—and now: she is going away from us
on the road,
is being swept away by the river.

III

LANDSCAPE
WITH RUINS

From *The Isenheim Altar*

IMPRESSION OF THE WHOLE

Grünewald, green wood; green is the wood of fever
where the paths founder under rustling arches.
By following your footsteps, can we ever traverse it?
Will we, disarmed passersby, survive
the disquieting crossroads, baleful clearings?
Save ourselves from ambush, drive back the ghosts?

And in the end, at the drenched awakening
from harsh shadows, psychedelic light,
will we hold your hope close like a diaphanous rose?
Or does only a bit of dank clay
await us among the rotted leaves
that give off the smell of all decay?

THE PLACE AND THE TIME

Their faces marked with the colors
of autumn, with livid spots
and scarlet streaks (wild
painters, the plague, syphilis
rivaling your nightmares); they stream out
of fever hospital and almshouse,
the unfortunates of Isenheim, carried
on the backs of robust
silent monks, or they stump along
with crutches and staffs—
the crippled, the mutilated,
the blind, too, caught
in an eddy of signs and clumsy
shuffling, stretching their hands
toward their companions, asking
"Where is the altar of Mathias?"—
one day they found themselves before these images.
Like mist a formless prayer
rose from their tears, a prayer suffused
with pestilential breaths and groping gestures,
and the God who scrutinizes hearts
loved it like the sweetest liturgy.

This happened in the beginning,
centuries before tourists burst
into a museum, behind garrulous guides,
and Paul Hindemith meditated
musically on *Mathis der Mahler*.

CRUCIFIXION

At this crossroad of darkness
you rise huge before us,
dry tree, steelyard
supporting the big inert body.

A bare cross-plank
cuts across space;
a bare vertical one
soars above time:

Cartesian axes
of life and death,
around which the black four-leaved
clover now opens wide.

In the lobes above, emptiness and terror
as in the cry "My God
why hast thou forsaken me?"
Below is all human grief
made rock in three figures.

But behold: the victorious Lamb advances
toward his wounded counterpart.
And a peremptory Prophet shows us
salvation in the metaphor!

Deposition

The silence is too great: not even
your lament breaks it, Magdalen.
It is better to veil your face entirely
like the mother, or lower it palely
in mute compassion, like the disciple.

The battle is over. Nothing
disturbs exhausted nature anymore.
The earth that shook in the ninth hour
lies still now

like the short stone rectangle
prepared to receive the one
who bore for us the avalanche of wrath
and is free now among the dead.

ANNUNCIAZIONE

Piomba il falco dal cielo, non colomba—la colomba è lei,
    spaventata,
che distoglie lo sguardo e vorrebbe nascondersi
e congiunge tremante, quasi a difesa, le mani.
Intorno a lei sembra svuotarsi il mondo.
Solo una luce pallida, di nebulosa lontana,
tinge di fuori le vetrate; ma qui, nel più riposto
oratorio, sotto le oscure volte,
arde della sua essenza l'invasore arcangelico,
fiamma le ali e il manto, oro la bionda testa.
Il tempo, lacerato dall'annunzio imperioso,
scorre come i pesanti drappeggi, i due sipari
tra i quali l'alto dramma ora comincia a svolgersi.
E già nel solco dell'umile resa
cade il seme divino, ed alla terra arida
la radice di Jesse prepara il suo virgulto.
Con ignota dolcezza e ignota pena
la giovinetta chiusa nell'ascolto
sente stormire in sé i giorni futuri.

ANNUNCIATION

The falcon—not the dove—plummets from heaven;
she, the frightened one, is the dove,
who averts her gaze, wanting to hide
and, trembling, joins her hands as though
to defend herself. The world seems to empty
around her. Only a faint light, far off and hazy,
dyes the stained-glass windows from outside;
but here, in the most secret oratory, under the dim vaults,
the archangel invader glows with his essence,
his mantle and wings flames, the blonde head gold.
Time, rent by the imperious announcement,
flows like the heavy draperies, the two curtains
between which the lofty drama starts to unfold.
Already the divine seed falls into the furrow
of the humble surrender, and the root of Jesse
prepares its shoot for the arid ground.
With unknown sweetness, unknown pain,
the young woman lost in her listening
feels future days rustle deep within her.

Celestial Concert

All the music we have heard
and all that we have dreamed
rises here in luminous figures.
They unfurl great wings, don rose-white
or flaming garments, cover themselves
with green feathers, like young buds,
wear halos of gold and emerald.
They have turned into angels
that touch lute and viola
with radiant fingers. They descend
toward us, a wavy stream, throwing off
sparks. Around them everything is music:
the pavilion with its light crenellations
poised overhead like trills, the decorations—
marble or leaves—interchanging, the sky
where all the colors wheel in a melodious rainbow,
mountain and shepherd's path,
blue castle and virginal lake,
and on its bank, closed in the secret
of its brown leaves, the rose burns.
Above all, she is music, the adored one,
lovingly gazed-at, in both the expectation and the fruit,
her transparent flesh veiling the spirit's fire
that kindles in the splendor of the Son.
At her feet even the simplest objects
are brightened by echoes and reflections: the cradle,
tub, the lowly pot
or a small jug . . . Will it be granted to us too
in an ineffable moment
to be nothing but light and music?

RESURRECTION

Like shipwrecked men, who have
barely survived the storm,
the three soldiers stand, terrified,
on the shore of night,

their useless swords
and helmets
reflecting the sudden gleam
of a violent light—

while, vivid meteor,
the Lord rises from the tomb
and darkness parts before Him
as once the Red Sea waves
parted before the Israelites.

Even more solemn are this new
passage, this new Moses
for a vaster people. The land of the dead
from which he comes is a darker Egypt,
and more dizzying than any dreamed Canaan
is the unknown shore toward which he precedes us.

AFTER ISENHEIM

And you, Mathias, an old man with the face
of Paul the Hermit but not his destiny—
the roads were long for you
after Isenheim, before Halle.
Heaped with honors at the start (disgust
soon seized you for the wicked
court splendors), in flight from then on,
mixed with the furious wave
of peasant rebels, or the weeping
defenseless mob driven from their homes
by the ruthless vendetta of the powerful.
A perpetual gallop of horses
over the devastated fields, hunger,
the wind of plague, and scattered everywhere
the seeds of death. What remedy
could the sweet humble herbs you sold to live
bring to the terrible wounds,
the fevers? Rue, marjoram,
and scented rosemary, the legacy
of your days with the monks at Isenheim.
Did you at least believe in that comfort?
Or did you see everything blow away
like straw in a storm? Did you still
set a goal to your tired wanderings?

The Fountain

Your dream of purifying! Since rain
washes the world, and springs
spurt swiftly
from its dark heart,

to prepare a basin that would receive
the innocence of water . . . With dolphins
playing, perhaps, or white birds
carved on its rim, and in the center
marble faces spilling a tireless murmur
from enigmatic lips.

Your never-achieved fountain, lost now
in the night with you! Only you
know its secret, you are its shell,
an ear perennially strained to listen

while, deep down, invisible veins
traverse the nameless earth
enclosing the one
who was Mathias Grünewald—
in a pit of plague victims,
outside the walls of Halle.

A Farewell

Il pacchetto in cui restano ancora
due sigarette. La lettera
cominciata e non finita.
Il tubetto di dentifricio spremuto a metà.
L'impronta da spianare in un letto
dove non sarà impressa mai più.
In quante semplici cose
si annida un prima senza poi,
che soltanto lo scatto delle forbici
fatali ci rivela!

to L, to a shadow

The package with two cigarettes
left in it. The letter
begun and never finished.
The half-squeezed tube of toothpaste.
The hollow to smooth out in a bed
that will never again bear your imprint.
In how many simple things
a before with no afterward lurks,
to be revealed to us only
by the fatal scissors-snap.

Sono morti
anche i tuoi abiti nell'armadio, le tue scarpe sotto il letto,
morto il tuo posto a tavola.
Nei vecchi taccuini la tua scrittura
è geroglifico d'un incerto elisio.
Tutte le tue fotografie
hanno, di colpo, mutato espressione.

La casa stessa è strana, alterata ed ignota.
Per ogni sua parete passa il confine—
in ogni stanza
l'oscuro fiume e il barcaiolo invisibile
che ti ha portato di là,
mentre a noi ancora rifiuta il traghetto.

Even your clothes are dead
in the closet, your shoes under the bed.
Your place at table too.
Your handwriting in old notebooks
is a hieroglyphic of an uncertain Elysium.
All the photographs of you
have suddenly changed expression.

The house itself is strange, different, unknown.
Through every wall the boundary passes—
in every room
the dark river and the invisible boatman
who carried you off
but still refuses to ferry us across.

How regal death is!
The people who would have
joked lightly with you yesterday, today stand
timidly, whispering, full of compunction,
staring bewildered at that haughty marble prince
you suddenly turned into.

Even the children and I have been granted
a kind of crown:
not the big one but the kind suited
to someone sitting on the throne steps.
In your honor we too receive
our share of honor,
until the solemn procession breaks up and everyone,
after the last handshake and nod, goes back
to his small beloved, living world,
leaving you to your final fate
and us to the reflections of your ice.

They're wise, the Polynesians,
who lay their dead in canoes, push them
into sunset waters, entrust them
to a course some god or other will steer.

For the sea washes away all errors and pain,
wipes out all regrets with rare metamorphoses,
and consoles for the lost past, the future never to be,
offering in their place the likeness of its foam.

Dead, you too crossed the sea
when we took you back to your island.
On the ship that night I listened to the water's voice,
imagining its white wake,
and felt that you were pure now and at peace,

and I was happy that by sheer chance
our route was the same as the sun's route
and the land where you were born
was western land—the quietest,
in whose womb doves sleep.

Are you already used to death?
Or is it hard for you to wear,
like a new suit that doesn't yet
quite fit your body?

Do desires rack you,
ragged threads of regret show?
Does remembering tug at you with its noose?
Or was your surrender to your icy garment
sudden and effortless?

Your body that lay next to mine
rots now in the ground. In this
stupendous lonely spring
that explodes above your death,
through you I feel a kinship with every clod,
with every clump of daisies.

How far are you
from the small moon
that still wanders over the western mountains?

Is red dawn
still in the east for you?

If I took as one compass arm
that pointed bell tower from which
a crow has plummeted,
like a bundle of black rags,
in what direction should I revolve
the other arm to look for you?

Does the equator exist for you?

From which meridian
does the invisible world begin?

How can I know your coordinates
when every sextant shatters,
every compass goes mad?

How docile are the dead.
From a single tender gesture,
lost in the desert,
they let us fashion an amorous garden.

Submissive, they put on every garment
with which wily memory clothes them;
they smile, obedient,
bow lightly to our illusions,

accept the role which we assign them
when we reinvent the past,
agree to everything, never rebel.
Their calm is beyond describing.

Perhaps it is simply great compassion
for us and our painful lies.
Even for them no disaffection
can stand up to the test of death.

The distance between the living and the dead
is no worse than that between
the living and the living. We know them
both already. It remains to be discovered
whether, when we are all lined up in silence,
feeding the flowers and the grass,
we will be any closer, or whether, in whatever
condition and wherever man finds himself
in relation to the rest, and to the frontier,
his solitude will shine forever on the zenith,
like the last star of the frosty Bear,
to indicate an unchanged North.

Dawn and a kind of gray pity
glide over your absence.
Tonight in a dream I hated you. Even that
brought you to life.

The Clock

This circle that once contained time,
its imperceptible ticking, its light steps
moving toward simple earthly goals
(a vacation or a homecoming, a carefree adventure
or a planned meeting of old friends),

now holds a frozen gesture
that nothing interrupts anymore, does not vary or erase itself:
a gesture like that of a marble angel
on a tomb who lifts one arm high
to indicate the unknown
while the other points, decisive, to the ground.

Here among us, where is the face to match those arms?
Featureless, inexpressive, veiled,
it is only the face of a blank sky, a plain
that exhales vapors and miasmas in the August sultriness.

Searching for an answer, we stare futilely at clock faces
on which never again will we read
a different hour.
Death has built a nest in all our clocks.

Innocent travelers, who will be expected
vainly at stations in all the cardinal points,
have reached another destination, the last one,
without ever having left.

The Explosion and the Digging

If the world must end in a roar, this has been a valid
   rehearsal.
The city has trembled; for terrible instants its streets have
   seemed those of a crazed anthill.
But the silence to which the roar suddenly changed, for too
   many, dismayed us more than the roar.
More than the flame, its companion on that ripe August
   morning,
the immediate night that had engulfed too many appalled us.
More than the landslides and cave-ins among which we dug
   ceaselessly,
the solid immobility we too often sensed beneath them.
More than the scorching heat in which, exhausted, we
   struggled to find someone who was alive,
the ineradicable chill of too many of our discoveries.
And more than the deformed bodies which we unearthed in
   the midst of the slaughter,
the deformed souls that had conceived and willed it.

Caino e Abele (I)

Caino disse ad Abele: « Vieni con me nei campi ».
E quando un poco ebbero insieme camminato,
gli si avventò col suo bastone, un grosso ramo senza fronde,
dove soltanto nodi aguzzi sporgevano.
Fu quella la prima arma, così poco sofisticata,
eppure in sé già tutta conteneva
la sua posterità di frecce spade pugnali
e fucili e cannoni, bombe e valige di tritolo,
perché fu sufficiente a aprire un varco alla morte.
E la morte comparve sulla terra, scendendo
lungo le vene di Abele, come la vita
vi era discesa dai lombi di Adamo:
la prima morte della terra, che fu morte violenta
e ruppe il corso naturale delle cose
ancor prima che questo fosse stato avviato.
La violazione precedette l'ordine:
e Adamo nel declino che su di lui incombeva
(morte morieris), lento consumarsi
della sua umana cera, su cui la fiamma
s'indeboliva piano, vide ad un tratto spento
il suo figliolo più giovane,
e pianse insieme l'uccisore e l'ucciso.

CAIN AND ABEL (I)

Cain said to Abel: "Come with me into the fields."
And when they had walked a little way together,
he fell upon Abel with his cudgel, a thick branch
that had been stripped of leaves, and bristled with sharp
    knobs.
That was the first weapon, not sophisticated,
yet in itself it already contained
all its descendants: arrows, swords, daggers,
guns, bombs, suitcases filled with explosives,
because it was enough to open a way to death.
And death appeared upon the earth, descending
along Abel's veins, as life
had descended there from Adam's loins:
the first death on earth, a violent death
that shattered the natural course of things
even before it was established.
Violation preceded order, and Adam,
in the decline that weighed on him
(morte morieris), a slow consuming
of his waxen face, in which the flame
paled slowly, saw the younger of his sons
dead suddenly, and wept for the slayer and the slain.

Cain and Abel (II)

When Abel received the fatal blow, the same astonishment
and terror invaded both young faces for an instant,
that of the standing youth and the one struck to the ground,
as though both were incredulous about what had just
    happened.
Then a wan peace suffused the face of Abel,
the mysterious snow that erases all expression.
But Cain's face hardened in a desperate
and dark refusal: "Am I my brother's keeper?"
while deep inside him a voice kept crying: "You are his
    murderer.
And this earth that has opened its mouth to drink
the blood of Abel, shed by you,
you will try to flee from it, flee from everyone,
but you will not be able to flee from yourself.
Blood—no matter where you go; your paths
and your children's paths will be blood-soaked.
From blood's first star a whole firmament will be born."

CAIN AND ABEL (III)

"Because of you, earth will be cursed,
the rivers dry, and every clod polluted;
the fields of wheat will turn to fields of bones.
Like night, on which you model your furtive footsteps,
you will walk through the world, but your brand
is a brand of fire; and darkness cannot erase it.
Abel's blood, the blood of all the slain,
cries out against you."

The Inventory

The young woman with the shattered spine, the burned
    children,
the eighty-year old man who should by rights have expected
to die peacefully in his own bed, not this absurd end,
the rubble of bodies among the rubble of walls,
the anguish of mundane objects: the eyeglasses, still intact,
the tabloids, a suitcase full of summer clothes,
small tin molds shaped like butterflies and flowers
that will never again be filled with sand,
all that our hands—torn by splinters of cement
and sharp twisted iron—have brought to light,
all that our eyes have seen and the mind finds it impossible to
    comprehend
because the human mind does not understand the inhuman,
all of this remains like an immense wailing
that rises from the very stones of this city
to implore justice. The dead are at peace now,
but without justice, what peace can there be for the living?

The Funerals

Here—gliding toward us from above—
are the ones who come punctually on the wings of death
and never miss a public funeral.
They make their gray appearance
like the last swift shadow of dusk
and leave as quickly. They have laid a flower
on the ground soaked by a rain of blood,
murmuring useless words, forgotten
before they reach any destination,
words no one could preserve inside himself even if he wanted
    to:
they are like air bubbles that burst as quickly as they form.
Their hands have reached for hands that pulled away.
Their ambiguous eyes have searched hesitantly
for other eyes, blinded by tears
or hard as stones, having wept themselves dry.
We have all rejected their pity
with our hearts, some of us aloud:
we need help to live, not to cry!
But meanwhile, among rows of the dead and of the
    nonexistent,
the space where ferocity rages keeps on growing.

IV

THE
IMMINENCE
OF THE
SEA

From *Hymn to Joy*

LE PAROLE CHE MI SCRIVI

Le parole che mi scrivi mettono foglie e fiori,
crescono intorno a me a formare
una deliziosa pergola.
È il mio confine del mondo, la dimora segreta
dove riprendo forza, nel faticato giorno,
e mi riparo dall'ardore sotto l'intreccio dei rami
così ariosi e leggeri—
attraverso cui guardo, di notte, dolcissime stelle.

The Words You Write to Me

The words you write to me put out leaves
and flowers, grow around me to form
a delicious pergola. It is my boundary
of the world, the secret dwelling-place
where I regain my strength in the difficult day.
And I shelter from the heat under the tangle
of branches, so light and airy, through which
I watch the lovely stars at night.

IL GIRASOLE

A quest'ora si desta il girasole
nel tuo giardino e volge il capo ad oriente
per seguire poi il sole nel suo giro
fino al tramonto, fedelmente.

Anch'io mi desto e subito rivolgo
a te il pensiero. L'amore è il mio astro,
di cui segna le ore, tutto il giorno,
la mia segreta meridiana.

SUNFLOWER

At this hour the sunflower wakes
in your garden, and turns its head
toward the East, from now on
to follow the sun in its course,
faithfully until dusk.

I wake too, and turn my thoughts
first thing in your direction. Love
is my star, its hours marked all day
on my secret sundial.

A Different Latitude

Now, mornings, the mists linger
because the tired sun has no wish to dispel them.
The ripe grapes will not stay on the vines for long:
the foliage is fading in the woods.

And you in the North, perhaps
already see bare trees, hear a gray wind
blow against your windows in the evening,
bringing a faint hint of frost.

Seasons will never be the same
for us, out of phase thanks to a handful
of parallels. Our fates pass each other
at the equinoxes. In the spring
I am ahead of you . . . Now, instead,
it heartens me to know
you are ahead of me by several steps:
I get ready to follow in your wake,
docilely entrusting myself, like you,
to those unknown but loving hands
that guide us beyond the year's night.

Our Gazes Meeting in the Moon

Even though distance makes it improbable, let's arrange
a meeting of our gazes in the moon.
For you it rises later (a different time zone)
and is often veiled by the fogs
the Gulf Stream brings you.
For me, instead, it moves, crystal clear,
in a Mediterranean sky.

Still, maybe in some instant we can gaze
at exactly the same point, from our far-apart countries,
and a profound joy will tell us
the encounter has taken place. Even the moon
will shine more happily, within the angle
of our glances, restored
to its ancient role of love-mirror
in this era of astronauts and rockets.

White Bird

You say: "Winter is a great white bird
that spreads its wings above its nest
and gives secret warmth to the eggs
ready for hatching . . ."
              Then I think
death too has long snowy wings
and with them, in its nest of earth, protects
the life that will burst forth more intensely.

And fear quiets down. At the approach
of the pale solstice, I thank you
for offering me this image.

From *Book of Stars*

MAP OF THE WINTER SKY

With the map of the winter sky you drew for me,
I will go out before dawn, into a square now empty
of men, and lift my eyes to meet
the stellar passersby, who slowly move
around the Pole of the Bear. Of the most glittering
I will ask: "Are you Rigel? Are you Betelgeuse?
Sirius? Or Capella?" still in much doubt
(such is my inexperience despite your help)
about the answer. Meanwhile I will think about
San Juan, for that will be the night of God,
after the night of the senses and the soul,
and the stars, recognized or unknown, for me will be
so many angels whose silent flight guides me toward day.
And I will also think of you who, equally absorbed,
are contemplating the same firmament from another parallel,
feeling, like me, an outer ice and inner fire,
while our hearts, so distant from each other,
and still prisoners of time, beat in unison.

Colore di Betelgeuse

Hanno il colore di Betelgeuse
(mi scrivi) i fiori che sono riuscita
finalmente a donarti. Tu che vedi
una Galassia in ogni fioritura
terrestre e un fiore in ogni stella, hai legato
così il mio dono al più amato, per me,
fra tutti gli astri, quello che tu stesso
m'indicasti quando Orione scalava
l'orizzonte autunnale. Nel nuovo autunno i fiori
saranno morti e il confronto avverrà
tra una presenza e una memoria, o forse
tra due memorie: chi può, infatti, dire
con sicurezza che sia ancora viva
Betelgeuse? Forse noi vediamo solo
quanto di lei ricorda il cielo, a lungo
attraversato dall'antica luce
rosata, in uno spazio così grande
che il viaggio continua, pur se la stella è spenta.
Ma resterà sempre nostro il fulgore
che abbiamo accolto, come l'altro, tenero,
dei fiori divenuti d'ombra. Che importa
il durare, se una risposta è suscitata
di vita a vita, luce a luce? Avranno
le nostre stesse anime il colore
di Betelgeuse. Così
di riflesso in riflesso si propaga
un amore che custodisce il mondo.

COLOR OF BETELGEUSE

They are the color of Betelgeuse
(you write me), the flowers I finally
was able to give you. You who see
a Galaxy in every earthly blooming,
a flower in every star, have in this way
linked my gift to the most beloved, for me,
of all the stars, the one that you yourself
pointed out when Orion was climbing
the autumn horizon. In the new autumn the flowers
will be dead, the comparison will be
between a presence and a memory, or perhaps
between two memories: who can, in fact,
say with assurance that Betelgeuse
is still alive? Maybe we see, of it,
only what the sky remembers, having been crossed
so long by the ancient rosy light,
in space so great the journeying continues
though the star is spent.
But the splendor given to us
will stay forever ours, like that other delicate one
of the flowers turned to shadow. Who cares about the lasting,
if a response is evoked
of life to life and light to light? Our own
two souls will have the color of Betelgeuse. In this way,
from reflection to reflection
a love spreads out
by which the world's preserved.

Seamen's Stars

The seamen's stars, Capella, Rigel,
lift shining heads above the waters
lashed by squall winds, while
the season rushes on. Goal
of what anxious glances that spy on them
as they issue from a cloud, the tremulous sign
on the storm-tossed mast. (And the heart
flies to the dreamed harbor.) Beloved stars,
I wish that you could help
all other navigation too; since such, always,
is man's life, between the shore of birth
and that of death. Often
the invisible waves are wilder,
thicker with shipwrecks, than that sea
to which you bring hope. Nor is there
any signal unless man finds it
in his inner sky, and few are capable
of that: the saint who possesses
his soul in charity and prayer;
the innocent child who first
unfurls his sail; and the gentle
faithful lovers who have been,
to one another, rudder and star.

Gemini

They appear above the pine tree
that hides the East from me,
the bright Dioscuri. Side by side
they advance toward the cedar
beyond which they will set,
and a peaceful wake follows their course,
like silent music or a smile
that spreads across the skies'
immortal face. How pleasant
is my watching then, while the soul
opens to such beauty and, as though
it were another sky,
feels traversed as well by the ray
of the two serene stars.

ALTAIR

Anche tu resterai fra i miei tesori
più diletti—da quando in un notturno
giardino silenzioso (dolce l'erba
ai miei passi come dolce la mano
che mi guidava e sosteneva) a un tratto
in uno squarcio tra le prime nubi
d'autunno, sopra un lungo stelo
di tenebre, ai miei occhi
stupefatti ti apristi,
fiore di luce, Altair!

ALTAIR

You too will remain one
of my dearest treasures from the time
when, in a silent nocturnal
garden (the grass was gentle
to my footsteps as the hand
that led and supported me),
suddenly, in a rent among the first
autumn clouds, on a long
stalk of darkness, before my
astonished eyes, you opened,
flower of light, Altair!

FOMALHAUT

E' così breve il tuo soggiorno
sopra questo orizzonte (latitudine
quarantadue gradi nord), così frequenti
le nebbie e nubi che intercettano
con un velo autunnale
il tuo volto radioso
che quando mi è concesso scorgerlo
dalla finestra a cui veglio gran parte
delle mie notti, sento un dolce slancio
d'allegrezza, come chi dopo lunga
attesa veda infine giungere
l'essere amato—pur con un sospiro
per il nuovo imminente addio.
                                    Così
si volge il nostro rapido e segreto
convegno equinoziale, Fomalhaut.

FOMALHAUT

So brief your stay
above this horizon (latitude
forty-two degrees North), so frequent
the mists and clouds that hide
your shining countenance
with an autumn veil,
that when a glimpse of you is granted me
from the window where I watch,
many of my nights,
I feel a gentle rush of happiness,
like someone who, after long waiting,
finally sees the beloved one,
though with a sigh for the farewell to come.
                  Just so
our quick and secret
equinoctial meeting, Fomalhaut.

Sibilla Persica

O città dell'Oriente, Ninive dagli aerei giardini,
Babilonia fasciata di porpora, Ecbàtana superba,
Persepoli abbagliante di marmi, io tutte vi conobbi
quando vagavo nella pianura tra i due fiumi
e vedevo i peccati dei vostri re
e leggevo nel cielo la condanna
che li avrebbe seguiti. Ma così cristallino
era quel cielo che, nel contemplarlo,
per quanti segni vi scorgessi infausti
non mi sentivo turbata. Il futuro
già mi pareva un lontano passato,
uno sbiadito dolore pacificato da secoli;
l'attesa, uguale alla memoria: entrambe lievi
come il fruscìo di una siepe notturna,
esile crespa sul vento—e il vento un fiume
grande più dell'Eufrate, tutto recando
alla sua foce invisibile. Guardavo
luminose sospendersi le stelle
ai rami oscuri del cielo, la luna maturare
in un argenteo frutto e poi restringersi
in un frutto d'ombra. Era un prodigio l'ordine
naturale delle cose, più d'ogni folle cometa
che apparisse improvvisa, o di pietre infuocate
che dal cielo piombassero sul suolo
suscitando i miei vaticinii. Al tempo stesso
in cui li pronunziavo agli sgomenti
ascoltatori, restavo cosciente
di quella prima e ultima pace, inviolabile,
entro cui cade eterna la rugiada,
s'alza il canto dei grilli, stormiscono le foglie
al vento, mentre luna e stelle compiono
il loro corso. Ancora l'accoglievo
e n'ero avvolta, in una plaga intatta
dell'anima, di là dalla mestizia
dell'uomo al quale annunziavo il destino
dei suoi regni effimeri.

Persian Sibyl

Oh cities of the Orient, Nineveh of the hanging gardens,
purple-swathed Babylon, proud Ecbatana, Persepolis
gleaming with marbles, I knew you all
when I wandered in the plain between the two rivers,
saw the sins of your sovereigns,
and read in the sky the punishment
in store for them. But so crystalline was that sky
that when I gazed at it,
despite the ill-omened signs I read there,
I was not troubled. The future
already seemed to me a distant past,
a faded pain the centuries had soothed;
the expectation, equal to memory: both light
as the rustling of a nocturnal hedge,
thin ripple on the wind—and the wind a river
greater than the Euphrates, bearing everything
to its invisible mouth. I watched
the luminous stars hang
from the dark branches of the sky, the moon
ripen to a silver fruit, then shrink
to a shadow fruit. The natural order of things
was a marvel, more so than any mad comet
that suddenly appeared, or red-hot stones
that plummeted from sky to ground,
provoking my prophecies. At the same time
as I pronounced them to the dismayed
listeners, I remained aware
of that first and last peace, inviolable,
in which the dew falls eternally,
the song of crickets rises, leaves rustle
in the wind, while moon and stars complete
their course. I still welcomed
and was enveloped by it in an intact region
of the soul, beyond the melancholy of the man
to whom I was announcing the fate
of his ephemeral reigns.

Libyan Sibyl

How quickly the wind writes on water and on sand,
and quickly cancels.
But on sand, the marks remain
a little longer. I study them
from these dunes where I sit and where
it is an event to see how the shadow
of the slimmest stalk bends, and quartz and mica
shine white-hot like splinters of a burning-glass.
I sense a pattern. . . . But, solitary wayfarer
(stopping before me as before the Sphinx), do not ask me
about too distant goals. All the roads I can point out to you
continue on to pierce the horizon,
but nearly always lead to a mirage.
Then too my divination,
like your life, is a bitter game
willed by the gods, here in the desert.
I will never reveal to you anything
more than the handful of sand you lift,
then let sift thoughtfully
through your opened fingers, grain by grain,
the opaque grains of time, whose flow
is your flow. And it returns, this tiny bit
of sand, to lose itself in the other uncounted sands
from which you gathered it, turned for the moment
into your own hourglass. If you persist in questioning me
my glance will go blank, and this blankness will be the only
answer that surfaces in me. And still I tell you: "Persevere."
Whether you have come shipwrecked by a harsh
storm of the Syrtis, or undertook your journey voluntarily
in this inhospitable expanse, persevere, traveler,
to the very end, though you have
no other guide but your anxiety
and dismay. Truth awaits man,
but awaits him only
when his last step has been taken.

Phrygian Sibyl

I am close to the Beginning, for the Beginning
is from Zeus. I was, indeed, born on the mountain
sacred to him, Mount Ida, rich in forests,
where the wind resounds like the god's voice. Yet I feel
equally close to the end, that does not come from Zeus
but from the Fate mightier than Zeus that decrees death
for every living thing. Too many times I have witnessed
beginning and end. I saw nine flourishing cities
rise, then fall, one on top of the other,
their names like so many waves
quickly blotted out on the brief strip of land
that was mine. Only one, entrusted to a poet,
lives on in memory: such is the power of words.
But I weep not only for Ilium: I bemoan
all nine of the destroyed cities, their high walls
crumbled and burnt, now mingled with the rock
to form the skeleton of the hill of Hissarlik.
I weep for all their dead. Each had its Hector
and its Priam who, though unknown, reddened
with their blood rivers that mirrored leaping flames,
and on which so many bodies descended to the sea.
I weep for other cities in other lands
which calamity struck or will strike.
An ever-lengthening Zodiac of ruins
unwinds around the planet of man,
since the day he learned to mix hatred and pain
in his cup, a bitter drink with which he thought
to quiet his thirst for power. How many women's faces,
shrieking, imploring, have followed in turn
in my ageless face; what humiliated wisdom
has risen from my heart and entrails
across millennia, struggling to resist
the fierce madness that leaves
no room for pity. Countless victims
lament in me, and only this great lament
remains of most of them, turned to a root
deep in the earth from which my stem has risen.
Therefore I shall speak only of those women
who found fame along with disaster (a pallid

consolation, and none at all for them). With Andromache
I drew close to my man for the farewell,
showed him his small son, he too condemned to death
by the death of his father. I was Cassandra,
who twice—in a vision and in reality—
saw the violation of her city and her body,
but was powerless
to avert anything. I wrung my hands with Hecuba
on the deserted shore, her last son
lost by now, her old husband and king felled
like a tree trunk assaulted by the axe.
Emptied of tears, my eyes
were dry as the withered breast
that had nourished so many lives in vain.
A stony silence, more terrible
than a scream, enfolded everything.
The very world was stone; nothing else
reigned there.
        Only stone and spent embers
where Ilium's grandeur stood.

From *Rings of Time**

THE KNIFE THROWER

Such tremendous pains pierced
my chest that I thought
of a knife thrower, and suddenly
I saw him there before me.
With icy eyes he was hurling his knives
at me; they all hit their target.
Though no blood dripped,
I felt I was dying all the same,
and by this time only begged him
to finish me off.
But with the last knife in his lifted hand,
he slowly lowered it, with an evil smile,
and said: "No, I want to save this
for another day,
when it will take you unawares."

*Unpublished.

ANNIVERSARY WITH AGAVES

This day, one of love and laceration
so many years ago, finds us walking together,
over sand and rocks, your hand
helping me in the difficult places
and your gaze directing mine toward
the high barrier of agaves and reeds,
the northeast boundary of the beach.
"See," you say to me, "here they are," and point out
the five agaves ready,
after almost a century of waiting,
for the incredible flowering. Closed
in its great brown egg, each phoenix-flower
is preparing to break into
ecstatic flight: the brief nuptials
in sun and wind, celebrated by swarms
of golden bees—then, immediate death.
We watch the agaves stretch
to their fulfillment
in the indomitable straining of their stalks,
and the surrender of the already spent leaves, that sacrificed
all their sap to the one end, and now fold up
like lowered sails. Something in us
deeply, almost desperately, responds
to that straining, that surrender.
I feel a lump in my throat and remain
silent. You say softly: "Even plants
have their destinies."

Breathing on the Mirror

I breathe on the mirror
so that my face dims and fades.
I try in this way to get accustomed
to the time when it will be only mist.

Or I move my fingers in the wind
as though they were pale leaves
of those future bushes
that will grow from my body.

Who knows, I wonder, if then
it will be sweet or frightful.
Or if it will only seem to me
I have always been dead.

EURYDICE

to the poet Febo Delfi, in memory of Maria

Don't be angry at yourself if day's sweetness
steals into you once more, if you smile involuntarily
at the first sun that lightly touches your eyelids.
And suddenly the memory of those dear eyes, closed in
     death,
that can no longer see it,
wrenches your heart . . . Those eyes
now seek it through your own; the lovely body
in which you took delight, still stirs
in your remembering blood, the mysterious silence
dissolves in your song, Febo: because,
though invisible, the dead respond to life.
You know that with her airy step Eurydice
followed Orpheus, and—even more—the gleam
that faintly showed beyond him,
but always less faintly, at the cavern's mouth,
already announcing the warm world
by which she was attracted. If only Orpheus
had looked steadily at it! As long as we love life
we bring with us, in our wake,
every loved being. But if our glance,
like that of Orpheus, turns back
(no matter what the impulse) toward icy darkness,
inexorably in that instant
we restore to Hades all its power
over its present prey—and over us.

Cueva de las Manos

Brother humans, who lived
ten thousand years before us, on the steppes
of Patagonia, hunting the guanaco
and nandu, taking refuge at times
in caves like these from cruel
Southern storms, blowing from the Straits
(not yet Magellan's), how the heart
throbs at the discovery
of these prints of yours, these hands
that reach to us from the depths of time!
The imperious gesture halts us. And yet
we can't interpret it. Is it
a joyous greeting? Or the desperate
last farewell of castaways submerged
by the wave? Which of those opposed messages
was in your mind? Or was it still another: a rite, a game?
You can offer us everything on your
open palms and we will welcome it,
without forcing your enigma in any one
direction. Since almost certainly
your life must have known joy
and tragedy, like every life, like ours,
here we are too, in a reciprocal offering,
holding out to you what we are: transitory
like you, and so menaced
(though by different forces) that perhaps
in future nothing will be left of us,
not even a faint imprint in a cave.
Speak for us, then. We are leaves
of your same tree, torn off
by the same gust of autumn wind
that drives everything in a diagonal
much like the one you traced. And in the sky
the very same stars that shone
above your fall still shine
above ours, nor were they ever
aware of you, of us:

our world a speck invisible
from their distance, and not even a tick
of their immense time the interval
of those ten millennia that divide us.

Notes

Neurosuite

For Us No Mirror
gnothi seautón: "Know yourself." This sentence was written on the front of Apollo's temple at Delphi.

Slavic Notebook

Proščansko Jezero
Korana: A river fed by a series of fifteen lakes of which Prošče is the first, the highest, and the most solitary.

The Isenheim Altar

Mathias Grünewald (c. 1475–1529) was German. He painted a number of altarpieces, but his acknowledged masterpiece is the Isenheim polyptych, painted in 1515 and now at Colmar in Alsace. The fountain, Grünewald's last project, was never realized. Grünewald is the subject of Hindemith's *Mathis der Mahler*.

The Bologna Clock

On the morning of August 2, 1980, an unknown terrorist deposited a suitcase filled with explosives in a corner of the second-class waiting room of the Bologna railroad station. The explosives were connected to a timing device. Because it was the height of the summer vacation season, the station was very crowded. The explosion took place at 10:25 A.M., the hour at which the hands of the station clock stopped. That image, reproduced ad infinitum in all the newspapers, became a symbol of the terrible event. The number of dead and wounded was very high, far and away the highest that had ever resulted from a terrorist crime in Europe.

Cain and Abel (I)
morte morieris: "Thou shalt die by death."

Book of Stars

Map of the Winter Sky
San Juan is Saint John of the Cross, the great Spanish mystic, author of the famous treatise *Dark Night of the Soul.*

Color of Betelgeuse
Because it is at such a great distance from the earth, light from this star, sent out very long ago, continues to be visible, though the star is extinguished.

Seamens' Stars
From ancient times until now, human navigation has been oriented by the stars. Capella and Rigel are the biggest and the most brilliant.

Gemini
This constellation's chief stars represent the twins Castor and Pollux, the Dioscuri, sons of Zeus.

Altair
Altair is the principal star of Aquila.

Fomalhaut
This star is visible on the Italian horizon, in not-too-high latitudes, only for a brief period around the time of the autumnal equinox.

A Book of Sibyls

The Sibyls represent a very ancient and primitive form of cult, bound to the earth and to the vital forces that issue from it. They are mysterious figures. Even their number is uncertain. Heraclitus, who was the first to use the term, and Plato speak of only one Sibyl. Later they were considered to be numerous, perhaps because many places wanted to have a Sibyl of their own, and by late antiquity the number had gone up to seventeen. Lactantius, a Christian writer who lived between the third and fourth century, lists ten Sibyls, each with her place name, and it is to this list that Guidacci confined herself.

Persian Sibyl
The "plain between the two rivers" is obviously Mesopotamia, between the Tigris and the Euphrates, where some of the most famous peoples of antiquity lived: the Assyrians (capital Nineveh), Babylonians (capital Babylon), Medes (capital Ecbatana), and the Persians (capital Persepolis).

Libyan Sibyl
The waters of the Gulf of Syrtis were much feared as dangerous to navigation.

Phrygian Sibyl
The Phrygian Sibyl is also called the Trojan Sibyl and is sometimes identified with Cassandra, Priam's unfortunate daughter, to whose all too correct prophecies no one listened. Guidacci has associated her also with the two tragic Trojan women Andromache and Hecuba, respectively the wife and mother of Hector.

Hissarlik is a place where, thanks to the faith and generosity of Heinrich Schliemann, traces were discovered of the Homeric city. The hill was found to contain superimposed remains of no fewer than nine cities, which had been built and destroyed in succession. One of the intermediate strata was the Trojan city.

Rings of Time

Cueva de las Manos
Guanaco and nandu are animals depicted in many Patagonian caves.

Chronological List of
Principal Publications

1946   *La sabbia e l'angelo*
       Vallecchi, Firenze

1956   *Giorno dei santi*
       Scheiwiller, Milano

1965   *Poesie*
       Rizzoli, Milano

1970   *Neurosuite*
       Neri Pozza, Vicenza

1973   *Terra senza orologi* (Quindici poesie e sette disegni)
       Edizioni Trentadue, Milano

1976   *Taccuino slavo*
       La Locusta, Vicenza

1977   *Il vuoto e le forme*
       Rebellato, Padova

1980   *L'altare di Isenheim* (also contains *Un addio*)
       Rusconi, Milano

1981   *L'orologio di Bologna*
       Città di Vita, Firenze

1983   *Inno alla gioia*
       Nardini, Firenze

1986   *Liber fulguralis* (translated by Ruth Feldman)
       Facoltà di Magistero, University of Messina

1987   *Poesie per poeti*
       Istituto di propaganda libraria, Milano

1988   *Una breve misura* (haiku)
       Vecchio Faggio, Chieti

1989   *A Book of Sibyls* (translated by Ruth Feldman)
       Rowan Tree Press, Boston